Tides of Fancy
(Poems)

Eunice Ngongkum

Langaa Research & Publishing CIG
Mankon, Bamenda

Publisher:
Langaa RPCIG
Langaa Research & Publishing Common Initiative Group
P.O. Box 902 Mankon
Bamenda
North West Region
Cameroon
Langaagrp@gmail.com
www.langaa-rpcig.net

Distributed in and outside N. America by African Books Collective
orders@africanbookscollective.com
www.africanbookscollective.com

ISBN-10: 9956-551-71-6

ISBN-13: 978-9956-551-71-2

Table Of Contents

Preface

Poetry, a genre of literature which elevates the writer's thoughts and feelings about the realities of his or her environment through the beautiful exploration of language, verse and meter, has gained ground as a medium of expressing what can hardly be conveyed more accurately through other genres of literature.

In consonance to this, Eunice Ngongkum, in this collection, *Tides Of Fancy (Poems)* depicts a landscape where norms of human and social behaviour have been shelved and where many, a dishonest—supposed to be dispenser of moral values—adorns the thrones of deceit, betrayal and other deviances.

The collection of forty- two (42) poems derides prevailing behavioural patterns which all, from the learned to the man on the street, are supposed to eschew. With a content that reflects humanity as a whole, the poet has discarded the myth that poetry is not for the ordinary man! She draws from ordinary experiences and going by the aptness of the titles and peculiarities of the content, she articulates her thoughts and vision in free verse, occasional structural inversion, visible rhythm, rhyme and concrete images. The lead poem, "I Speak Still", echoes the keynote, and canalizes the poet's motivation, vis, "writing to instil hope and courage in sundry souls."

The proliferation of themes and other issues of moral concern, drawn from diverse backgrounds in colourful language and expression, bears testimony to the richness and profundity of the writer's experience and creative imagination. The poems are replete with undertones of moral prescriptions. She shuns hypocrisy, betrayal, cruelty, interpersonal conflicts, waywardness, warped consciences, indecency, abuse of power, insensitivity to the hurts of others and other vices which have made man more contemptuous of others and his environment. She envisages a society grounded on hard work, living for others, genuine love, moral responsibility, love for one's country, etc. The poet is convinced that our rejection of core human values diminishes our present, fertilizes discord, creates chasms and sows seeds of destruction for our future. The varied subject matter is thus a guidepost intended to reshape human thinking from the hitherto warped conceptions which engender baseless human hurts, frustrations, depressions and unnecessary tangles.

Conscious of the craze for thorny beauty, lofty sophistication, unfounded gains, cosmetic achievements and votive self-exaltation which adorn modern man's existence, *Tides Of Fancy (Poems)* is a milestone prescription for a rethinking of attitudes and perception. Eunice Ngongkum craves the reader to sow today appropriate seeds of vision for a healthier tomorrow. The ordinary themes treated, the diversity in subject matter, beautiful twist in language marked by modest expressions, subtlety in tone, the doubts and surprises expressed, the moral undertones, etc., are ingredients that spice the poet's craft.

The collection is a ready delicacy for the voracious appetite of every reader; both the pleasure seeker and the scholarly, will find in it diverse perspectives from which to draw conclusions.

Njikang Peter Mejame
Educationist, PLEG

THE CHARGE

The charge was flipped.
do write some lines
on sweating sharp
in steady rain
in this done lane
so known as lame
by spiteful czars
who once did sit
on these same banks
and drank from guides
who nonstop toil
in ceaseless rain.

What else to say
but state the state
of passion found
in what is done
and done in ways
to grant delight
to God, to self
to fellow man.

I SPEAK STILL

Behold I speak.
In my absences I speak
in my presences I speak
studied interests make me speak
to engage striking sundry souls
in matters of mutual interests
regarding the contests of life.

To the lily-livered, unmanned
by bloodsuckers browbeating them
into perpetual dithering
before sharp stiff life battles,
I speak to arouse boldness
to hold out against vampires
and ransack the kingdom of gnomes.

To sanctimonious hypocrites,
sailing still under false colours
slogging snug in cupboards of love
fudging issues for sordid gains,
I speak tough truth unvarnished
taking the wraps off treachery
to deliverance bring deceived souls.

To you straight from the shoulder friend,
keen our world to build on green truth
to restore dogged sanity
in the face of scorn and strong strife,
I speak support to decent duels
meant to liberate our people
from the custody of hellhounds.

My absences speak still
my presences speak still
speaking torch untouched spirits
to tone in with needed rightness
to fashion a fresh wholesome world.
Hurrah! for speaking presences
Hurrah! for speaking absences.

PAY ATTENTION

Give wings to your words, dear friend,
that they may scale the rooftops
to landcrash on the bull's eye
you aimed at when you spoke.
For words our minds do debag
laying bare our true designs
towards friend and foe alike.

Give thought to your words, kinsman,
lest they be words that destroy
the tiny seed of thin hope
we nurse in frail humanity.
Let them be words of thunder
putting teeth to firm resolve
to construct a just new world.

Pay attention to your words
lest you turn around in shame
when they come back bearing fruit
from words spoken oft in haste.
For words have full faculty
to create worlds unknown to us
outcome of the words we use.

IF RIVERS COULD SPEAK

If all these rivers could ever speak
they would our secrets publish abroad
secrets of clans, secrets of people
secrets foul, secrets to blow one's mind
secrets of self, secrets of nations
open secrets, smoothly kept secrets
if all these rivers could ever speak
they would such secret secrets reveal.

The rivers through the boonies meander
calmly with their cumbrances moving on
gathering the silt of more secrets
the rivers run on, deaf to our itching ears
the rivers run on, blind to our cheap thirsts.

TIDES OF FANCY

Each heart knows its own agonies
each heart knows its own bitterness
each heart knows its own aching aches
each heart knows its own stabbing sores
each heart knows its own tearing tears.
Let your own heart bring you comfort
as you these tides of fancy snag.

Each heart plays ball with its own picks
each heart knows its own regalements
each heart decides its own driveway
each heart bearhugs its own pieces
each heart pursues its own plain peace.
Let your own heart bring you real rest
as you this sound sluice of words hug.

VENTURESOME MINDS

Venturous runs excite the mind
daring the soul delights to find
venturesome minds fear not the mines
envisioned by souls full of pep
now a sure hit, at times a bust
teasing ball and chain prenotions
uncertainty curries notice
ready the venturous to vex
ever their wings of flight to clip.

Accolades pluck the ever brave
daring unplumbed worlds to explore
vitiate attendant pins and needles
enough, sated souls with glee to fill
new visions once more to shoot for
tipping the scales in fortune's eye
ushering in just the ticket
ready the soul once more to warm
ever so nigh to blessed bliss.

I WOKE UP

I woke up in darkness today
the darkness that salts my heart's wounds
sends it flying to freedom's field
for welcome rest in a sour world
I woke up in darkness today
and thought it time to clear out the mess.

I woke up in darkness today
the darkness that rams my taxed head
gifts it the eye-blinding migraine
then the keen itch for a fast fix
I woke up in darkness today
And knew this putrid madness must end.

I woke up in darkness today
the darkness that churns my peaked gut
demanding endless backdoor trots
to assuage a harsh regimen
I woke up in darkness today
spurred, these dreadful jackboots to throw
off.

But you, two-faced bosom buddy
keen my life in your murk to own
put forward phony panaceas
in lieu of the fix to this ache
my resolve is open and shut
kissing off this rat's nest is now.

STRUGGLING TO BE ME

I was ridiculed simply for existing
when all I wanted was simply to exist
at no time did I lust after you, being you
nor lay hold of your safe spot to make it mine
to construct thereon my stable and storehouse
all I wished was just to be me and none else.
I fought the fight, walked the talk of our union
but these all failed my ipseity to fess up.
Then I your definitions of me passed up
and for ways and means sought my death to front off
but not just ridicule this time greeted me
as the goons of war were unleashed to drown me
and wipe out my name from your album of life
now my trophies in blood and violence I count
in this strife that comes from struggling to be me
your lark about tactics fail to rein me in
your unleashed arsenal cannot my being ban
you cannot kill my yen to simply exist.

WHAT A WORLD

The kingdom of hypocrisy sits on high
perched in the towers of high academia
ready its ugly fangs on the straight to sink
crush them to expunction to reign supreme.
they convulse with laughter with you in your face
but stab you in the back when your back you turn
colleagues with you daily work but roast you nights
as if your place they gain once you expire.
In this vicious world of clear duplicity
you seek friendship but encounter enmity.

The scepter of hypocrisy spreads venom
in the zones the sedulous warily trod
striving in dog-eat-dog terrain to survive
their shining essays the fiends further frustrate.
nescient of the furthest reach of willful ill,
they your steady progress profess to proclaim
but turn green out of sight gnashing tough teeth
at the marvel of you despite storming storms.
In this monstrous realm of real hypocrisy
you long for true rapport but glean only woe.

The crown of hypocrisy becomes the head
of small fry foisted on thrones they least deserve
by salacious favors and lineal leanings.
trapped in the trap of patent ineptitude,
they seek their sickness by sadism to screen
its tentacles nestled in every corner,
each spotlight flash blanches out its dark hideouts.
In this brutish branch of plain hypocrisy
you chase understanding but reap animus.

NO BULWARK

Fear sits in the doorway of my heart
like an uninvited eidolon
refusing to grant peace open doors.
Catechesis of calamity
drives my spooked heart and mind up the wall
constant doses of awful tidings
and negative updates on all days
are enough to kill the man in me.

You tell me prudence is a true shield
against the hate and death in these spheres
but prudence alone is no bulwark
here where, sure as hell, power drunkens
and the drunkard must needs by fear thrive.
All is done to set someone on edge
perturbed, the next hour might be the end.
This saps you, takes you out, it kills you.

You need grit to rise above terror
that's enough to back the man in you.

I, TOO, HAVE KNOWN PAIN

I, too, have known pain
the piping pain as the needle pricks flesh
letting slip its weakness, its misery
the urge to scream like a she-goat in throes.......
I, too, have known pain.

I, too, have known pain
the pain perceiving the infant deprived
of suck, of life, of all it takes to thrive
as mum in some strange sick bay is stuck up.......
I, too, have known pain.

I, too, have known pain
the shocking pain to learn your son just conked
wasted in this thinning war, this pail strife
in the prime of life, sole hope of firm folk.......
I, too, have known pain.

But One there is who knew this pain and more.......
when He that tree embraced my life to save
like a sheep led to rout He knew real pain
the peace to know even this pain He took
seals relief still in these days of mad dogs.

READING ME WITH YESTERDAY'S EYES

Reading me with yesterday's eyes, friend,
blurs your vision of the actual me.
Errors of judgment dog the senses
leaning on yesterday's special jaunts
to learn today's peculiar posture.
Yesterday's eyes warp today's detail.

As one day gives way to another
and is no kin the one to the next
so too have I moved on, compatriot
from where you and I met years ago.
It may be the same me before you
but old hat eyes blear today's tableau.

I no longer kowtow to you, pal,
for your canine teeth I now can spot
teeth that have torn my flesh these past years
you can read me with yesterday's eyes
if that coddles your rash ego, cheat.

SO EASY

So easy to think the worst of someone
so easy to be sold on a brother
when against that soul mate you nurse bad vibes.

Distraught by a sister's blatant red shift
matey I moved to tear off madness strips.
But fed fat on spiced pork pie about me,
all she spotted was my plain phoniness.
Plain sailing to think the worst of someone.

Over the moon for a long-lost brother
in vain I gestured his notice to net.
My good name before now called into question,
on his guard, he made light of my designs.
So easy to think the worst of someone.

A looming kinsmanly rift espying,
the boldness I took the vile bridge to bridge,
heedless of a sly fraudster's deviousness
to cash in on worthy efforts for gain.
So easy to take advantage of friends.

So easy to think the worst of others
so easy to ween weird thoughts of someone
when against that person you bear ill will.

STEWARDSHIP

The stewardship of true freedom
summons guesstimates of our own

The stewardship of real freedom
asks not for gain its lines to run

The stewardship of plain freedom
says my life on the line for yours

The stewardship of pure freedom
states my full freedom on yours rests

The stewardship of fair freedom
quests no plain plaudits for the self

The stewardship of frank freedom
seeks those smeared by humans to cleanse

The stewardship of blunt freedom
for doomed ecosystems contends

The stewardship of true freedom
for the hordes lost in wild wars fights

The stewardship of right freedom
is we for you and you for us.

MOTHER'S HEART

Survival grips her motherly heart
with familial fibres of caring care.
Survival, her offspring's life is meet
tyrannic fixes in the teeth to kick.
She weaves all in her daily duties
defying death in this dearthly dominion.

Sundry scourges her slick shots spoliate
intent upon teaching her, her station
but maternal instincts these defy,
the moth of loving fervour eats up
like time does an attractive costume,
paramount, survival of her child.

Inroads she carves out in terror's depths
her son to snatch from the jaws of death
her scion by right she knows must live
quotidian survival her mission,
she with staying power herself clothes
melding her all into battle lines.

Before you mum, dark distress is dawn.

EXCEPTIONAL LIFE

The life he lived
he knew for sure
was meant to meet
his people's needs
and so, he gave
himself the task
to do the deeds
certain to speak
of that great need
to make them see
the greatest need
of Christ the king.

And so he lived
to help them through
life's complex clues
in humble ways
he set the pace
leading the way
on how to live
in pointed ways
to torch the lives
of all he met.

Your example
stands tall today
inspiring us
to live with aim
in these dark days
when many live
for self alone.

We draw a leaf
from you great life
to move our world
to truth and good.

GREEN SPIRIT
(In memory of Wangari Maathai)

Foremost flame of our unique earth
tree hugger Wangari Maathai
now gone to be one with the earth
you untiringly held fort for
I salute you, ecowarrior!
Our forests you mothered mother
from the Ngong Hills to the Congo
standing high our timber trees
in the face of grasping power.

Truth to tyranny oft you spoke
taking a chance on its irksome ire
undaunted your green spirit crossed swords
with creepers of our biomass
bent on bleeding our bleeding boughs.
These you pasted with potent points
in conservation's combat zone
earning well-earned crowns of glory
while staging forest views with verve.

Your superb shot shines still
firing us for the big-time fight
safeguarding our neck of the woods.
I salute you, ecowarrior!

GOETHE INSTITUT SHA

Ich kam nach Deutschland mit null Deutsch
Ich kam nach Schwäbisch Hall
Ich fand die Menschen nett und klar
Ich fand Goethes Zunge.

Von Leiterin bis Lehrerin
von Verwaltung bis KuF-Büro
Tag für Tag immer pünktlich
bewirken sie unseren Erfolg.

Goethe Institut Schwäbisch Hall,
Du gibst mir eine neue Sprache
In der ich Kreativ sein kann
Ich gebe Dir diese Zeilen
als Dank für die geniale Arbeit.

Eunice NGONGKUM
Klasse B1.2. April 2014

RARE GEM

You make of us speakers of Deutsch
Stephanie Shlicker refined teacher.
Your smile pleasant, your pace perky
wishing away our doubts and fears
in strict confines of Goethe's tongue.
We who from diverse realms do hail
a motley lot of sundry folk
distinct of mind as day and night
we come our thirst for Deutsch assuage.

The class with graceful ease you rein
each segment of the lesson falls
relaxed, winsome like tasty wine
engaging e'en the coy and halting
Deutsch sprechen in einen Monat?
amazing yet so palpable.

Stephanie, you are a rare gem!

LOST FOR WORDS

Because he stopped for me in that alien land
I called down tons of blessings on him
because my swarthy hue did not knock him down
I blessed him as, I would, my own son.

Unable now my thoroughfare to nail down,
in that louring land so unlike mine
I was lost for words to put out a feeler.
From his niche he noticed my quandary
in quick haste rushed in to help me find my way
my carry-on also to carry
maximum succor to a lost soul his aim
in that land so tart to outcomers.
Stunned, I swelled, he snapped me out
the moment, making mincemeat of strait-laced walls
pitched in the heart of the cosmos
here we were one howbeit oft-trump'd sharp-cut shades.

My light-hued son stopped for me right there
in that land famed for its yellow biases
my nature a thing of no account
and because he stopped for me in that strange land
I blessed him from my swell swarthy soul.

TO A FALLEN PATRIOT

Lachrymose dues for a fallen hero
the people proffer, overwhelmed.
Ripples of emotion, ripples of fear
tear through the heart like swelling streams
our loss is unspeakable!

Meaningless our efforts to restrain you
dud tears our distress register
grey dawns fall through your death to hold at bay
for you, just one, in raw prime slain
keen a flag for home to raise.

Down on that star-crossed greensward down you went
like a murphy sack dropped in haste
we clutch the emptiness in our insides
gazing at your fervid fervour
tall like the Fako mountain

Allow us a leaf from your garland draw
our country with fealty to clothe
in this night of cruel jackals.

VICTIM
(To a friend lost in an accident)

God had saved you before
when you lay sorely sick
prey to often dreaded
tropical diseases
malaria, filaria
cholera, diphtheria,
maladies we dreaded
could your early exit,
without fail, blaze abroad.

But a madcap driver
dozing in a done truck
hauled you like a thin leaf
into those low ravines
by ill-famed Ebombé.
Spirited arrivants
hotfooted you, frantic
to a rundown hospice
but recklessness that day
had the ball at his feet.

Victim of marked disdain
of time-tested warnings
bellowed from our rooftops
IF YOU DRINK, DON'T DARE DRIVE!
IF YOU DRIVE, DON'T DARE DRINK!
or standard speed limit
sixty kilometers
every hourly drive
the life you choose to save

may well- nigh be your own.
Victim you were dear friend
of the wanton carnage
on our thin tragic roads.

TREACHEROUS SLIP

When I set out with you
I held nothing back, friend
I gave my all to go
all the way with you then
on the oft chancy path
of this rare enterprise.

When I launched out with you
I knew we would succeed
and trumpet our victory
from mountains of glory
bringing fame to our land
in all we did and said.

But your treacherous slip
like a bolt from the blues
tears through my distressed heart
amazed dear mate at how
you could stand me naked
in our own marketplace
like a wonder for blue eyes
good game for man-sized mouths
eager the dirt to dish
shamelessly about me.

I dug through my inside
to see where I wronged you
to merit such disgrace
but found nothing friend.
I retraced our done path
to see where I had slipped

but found nothing mate
save your brazen bent
to crush others for gain.

TURN-AROUND COLLAR

You intoxicated the gullible
we too had been intoxicated at some point.

You led them in mutiny against us
we too had been roused against others at some point.

They sang your praises blackballed beretta
we too had sung them impetuously at some point.

They could there and then go to bat for you
we too had been psyched up to die for you at some point

until the you native to you checked in
and the cheaters you wore for keeps let slip

we who had seen the real you at some point
so succused at your long-delayed unravelling

knowing your brazenness and sweet tooth for baseness
a trait you masked by design, turn-around collar.

DEBORAH

When men their devout duty ditch
in times of fervid brutishness
divine endorsement is woman,
sacrosanct pathways illumine
for a picked people blown adrift
by winds of demeaning rapport.

Deborah, doughty sainted Sibyl,
mouthpiece of the gracious true One
speaks to arms a blighted people
to squash Jabinic menaces
fruit of besotted transgression.
The summons to baulking Barak
champion in ultimo victory
spurned, Deborah takes control
steering the course of ordained gains.
Duty done, she leads in triumph
the chosen ones in pleasant praise
of Him who constancy rewards
while the land keeps her jubilee.

Deborahic fiats well in place
where soft men their pigeons despise.

JEWELLED LIVES

Bright petals of your jewelled lives
shine through the grim mesh of dark days
caught in the cabal of politicos
resolute our forests to auction
for hoarded accounts in Swiss banks
while scrawny existence efforts
are mocked by swiftly drained greenwood.

Brilliant treasured tenacity
holds fort for our tear-jerked forests
bending over backward daily
to clinch ecological equipoise
for a hassled people on queer street.

Our earth registers your essays
as you uphold sustainability kinsmen.
Our lushness in fulsome salaams
holds out bouquets of recognition
for all you who bravely pick the brains
of verminous horned vipers
hobnobbing with inured Judases
to mess our estate, courting
ecological ruination.

YOU ARE UNIQUE

Some say you are defined by marriage
they swear with degrees you are nothing
except you a married woman be.
But your you on the inside counts on.
You are who you are, steady woman,
by how you really define yourself.

Some say your office post defines you
they swear sans such note you are nothing
and this from a state we daily flog.
But woman, your aplomb, yours alone
says in the end who you are really
so bait no bait to think otherwise.

While afghans add a thing now and then
in self inventions from time to time
let none of these paradigms prove you.
For, woman, your uniqueness defines you.
You are who you are, handsome woman,
by how surely you define yourself.

MOKOLO MARKET

I have been through
the bumps and jerks
of scurrying scutters
screaming toddlers
and bustling buyers
by busy stalls
beating prices
in a scorching
Saturday sun
before a bronzed
brash buyam-sellam
brazen like a he-goat.

I have been through
the squeeze and sneak
of small-time thieves
straining for a snatch
from the purse of
unwary buyers
dissolving in tears
as pickpockets
spoil over spoils
in shameless view
of all close by.

I have been through
the jam and jab
of motorcars
with ear-splitters
for so-called horns
shriller than all

police sirens.
Dinning the din
of attack calls
porters, barrows
groan under dense
dark sacks, 'passage.'

Mokolo market,
simply awesome.

DOMESTIC ASSAULT

Emotional knocks to her confidence
her quotidian reality in this space
so obvious his sense of entitlement
full focus you need to offer it him
else obvious broken bones you court for love
domestic abuse has many faces.

Expected to route the route he hands down
you need that course with canniness to tread
else a flubbed trip and you are done for it
often, it is all about beef and sway
feeling biggest is all the name of the game
domestic assault has many facets.

A mollycoddle is all it oft takes
the fury to fan, the horde to provoke
rendered incapable by right to feel,
the bad eye his eye scares your being to death
off he stomps swearing the fire next time
domestic abuse has many faces.

Dumped, you with his rage and bluffing bluff feud
you wonder how you found yourself in here
corking control, intimate tyranny
one long-term liberty deprivation
say, under tyranny your breath you draw,
domestic assault has many facets.

PHONINESS

You held me to off the wall standards
losing sight of my humanity
When I your daft ideals failed to meet
you ran my failures into my face
making me feel guilty in the same stride
for not being the one you wished me be
Nothing I did was ever correct
there was always a top way to it
you made me feel small before our kin
in your censoriousness and plain scorn
you made me live plain hell here on earth.

You had the license to make errors
you made them and got away with them.
For me there was no such elbow room
I sought to please, while frazzling myself
until the phoniness became plain
it was impossible to please you, chum,
it was too much to meet your standards
standards which you, in person, flaunted.
I hugged the high road to love myself
and carve a niche of hope in the mess
of what our warm union had become.

THE ALTAR OF AGE

The altar of age steals up on you
its kismet ogling you in the face
here may you your youthful angst let drop
the strain to make camp for life with youth
and plain relief from its keen itch earn
age wraps up our craze with agelessness.

The altar of age our frailties flaunt
sides and sites from view shrewdly shield
as 'lookism' its toll on us takes
dispatching some to an early grave
caught in fleeting flukes of timelessness
age sure freezes our fad with good looks.

DEMAGOGUE

Your slide into irrelevance was plain the day we saw you,
your future with us in question the day we moved with the
beat
of our cherished project, the one you wrecked with impunity.
We naively thought we could variance send packing as we
moved on
in forging a shared destiny for us and our progeny
but the demagogue in you snuffed out the tiny flame of hope
we put out in the face of your pert ploys to make the deal
work.
Your elastic relationship with truth was a thing that soured
our rapport, we, born on this side where candor is our given
word.
Your unhinged prejudices a fluid vault of your callousness,
you maddened the mood at even the most mirthful mustering
of the clans under the baobab tree, our shared kismet to
perpend.
You were loud and we were cowed by your utter brazenness,
thief.
You intentionally outraged us with everything you did
until nothing here stroke one as being outrageous anymore.
A deeply religious code about the shepherd closed our mouths
as we willy-nilly watched you make light of our little licks.
Others for you were mere satellites orbiting around your sun
till the tide turned and your troublesome tactics were made
public
your irrelevance then broadcast to your freak kith and kin

I HAIL YOU

I applaud your greed fellow passenger
I hail your pettiness fellow tourist
on this distinct bus trip we both embus
to discharge duty calls, both you and me
your penchant for always having your way,
even in a bus, crest of hoi polloi,
betrays your knack for notice, you upstart.

I salute your studied puerility
resurrected to needle me to ire
in this public space sans pecking order.
You make a poor run at running me down
in your bid to showboat yourself in here
your failure to floor me on this thick turf
is no check to your head trip, parvenue.

Now, new spheres you snag your ego to sing
in this common spot where none calls the shots.
Your home, your spouse, your own, on stage, hard sold
no rest in this hang-up, yourself to trade
phone calls to serfs, dubbed servants, warts and all
deep details, from the dome of self, distilled
to plain folk fagged out by self-seeking boasts
clear drama draining to all and sundry.
Your apathy stocks your arriviste mien
raised on the wrong side of prized humaneness,
you stop at naught, upstart, yourself to hawk.

PARVENUES

Parvenus run the show in our skies
strutting around in rented raiment
presuming all in all to master.
Eager our existence to poison,
they espy treason in a mere laugh

For them the whip hand carries full weight
banish tact, banish alternate views
their know-how they judge is all to it.
Craving some high office to conserve,
they spot a breach of faith in a cough.

THEY SAY

They say lying is their stock in trade
they say to fib is their beaten path
baby-kissers in soft-soap vestments
ruin of our days in this triangle
and so they lied their quandary to hide
as brazenly as only they could
at not giving you your due till now
they said you only moved higher
from a position that never was.

They say fudging is their other side
they say to con is their true nature
our equivocal politicos
resolved our existence to poison
with scads and scads of spoof promises
in this somber state, this stomping ground
where prevarication is real art
able them in power for good to keep
oblivious that a lie's life is brief.

They say concocting tales is habit
they say breaking a promise is norm
for our superincumbent ranis
hot our lives on greed's altar to hawk
in occult kingdoms to reign supreme
and for your death, sham buck shots they sold
their misdeeds to hide, their face to save,
they said to pyemia you succumbed
the hangman's noose we know took your life.

GIVE THEM THE NOD

Bury the blasted bereaved they say
seems some slip of tongue but so well said
of a people dead on landing here.
Their mimic man blazes this abroad
as if tombed, we weren't, once
born into this stranglehold
called home, a coveted place to be.
The vice here chokes to the skies
shutting the door on proper action
we either take or shut our large mouths
give the nod to the barons in charge.
Standard here the bereaved to entomb
as walking dead we move and have being.
Our dead bury, we must, now and then.
Intricacies of the lying tongue
fail the muzzled truth to entrammel
the walking dead are dead while living
no need to inearth them all over.

SCENES OF LIFE

Scenes of life as we coolly drive by
haunt the eyes with flashes of fierce gloom
they our unspeakable anguish speak.
We drive to rude awakenings
to scenes of utter desolation
speaking our indescribable woe.

Why would life such scenes ever enact
in this land where mimic men take charge?
Why would ruined fences and roofless joints
with seeming finality greet us
in a full house of pure brawn and bones?
Why would such scenes keep on greeting us
as if our lethargy to deride
when we our fatherland can rebuild?

THE FACE OF TERROR

We see the face of terror every day
in the deadly perils we daily face
in this terrain we dare to call our own
our loved ones from us snatched by gun by fear
we see the face of terror every day.

We see the face of terror every day
in the deadly bombshells we oft endure
from seeming liberators and traitors
in this haven now a den of robbers
we see the face of terror every day.

But terror will sure someday have its end
when we as one rise up its stay to halt
its grim grip on our lovely land kick out
a fresh refuge for the brave and just seal
that new day, terror's face no more we'll see.

CREATING CHAOS

The lizards' visit, kid bro, was never a check
in our frantic rush to don arsenals
in this war of attrition, this basin war.
See them spread chaos in their wake, Vally,
in this valley once a bright spot for you and me
we create chaos, beloved, but have no plan for it.

The lizards come, dear one, for ant-infested faggots
that we brought home that season of dry bones
in this clash of confusion, this bucket war.
See them spread bright death, as they come, Vally,
in this dull dale now a dark spot for you and me
we create chaos, dear one, but have no dream for it.

The lizards are here, my bro, the lizards are here
the faggots are dry, but the lizards remain
in this strife of disunion, this kettle war.
See them spread shame as solatium, Vally,
in this crappy vale now a damned spot for you and me
we create chaos, comrade, but have no cure for it.

DEATH CAME CALLING

When death came calling
it summoned Covid-19 as its courier
in surprise midflight it took us unawares
bringing down, in its wake, old and young alike.

When death came calling
it turned our intimacy into a snare
standing us nude in the marketplace
our delusions dismantled, crushed in a trice.

When death came calling
it shredded our plain hubris beyond recall
to bring to light its sheer emptiness and woe.

When death came calling
it left word we could not do as we pleased
with our lives, our ways, our thoughts, our bizarre actions.
Our cities emptied themselves without constraint
we holed up behind closed doors for days on end
unable the bright skies outside to behold
for fear of death, our loud mouths by face masks shut.

When death came calling
the boss was here to say he had taken note.

THE KNEE ON OUR NECK

The neck-choking knee surges anew
now in brazen blaze for the world's eye
the knee on our necks these sundry years
the knee of county mounties our bane
the knee of grim power chokes to death.

The nape-strangling knee sluices afresh
primed its force in this season to stake
the knee that takes our lives, our loves, our all
the knee the crying shame of our world
the knee of cruel command crushes us.

No greater sin than power abuse
no greater sin than killing your own.

Take a knee your rage to register
take a knee against thick racism
take a knee for our brother George Floyd.

CREATE SAFE SPACES

Create safe spaces for the strapped
create safe spaces for the weak
create safe spaces for the crushed
create safe spaces for them to thrive.

The divers deeds of the fiercely greedy
drive sundry folk to the margins of being
microaggression the run-of-the-mill,
raises the roof for thoughtful endeavors.

Create safe spaces for the trapped
create safe spaces for the lorn
create safe spaces for the poor
create safe spaces for them to bloom.

The sore engine of inequality
strives some out of existence to root out
their piddling engagements to hold the fort
callously crunched by jackboots of power.

Create safe spaces for the treed
create safe spaces for the fleeced
create safe spaces for the conned
create safe spaces for all to grow.

Printed in the United States
by Baker & Taylor Publisher Services